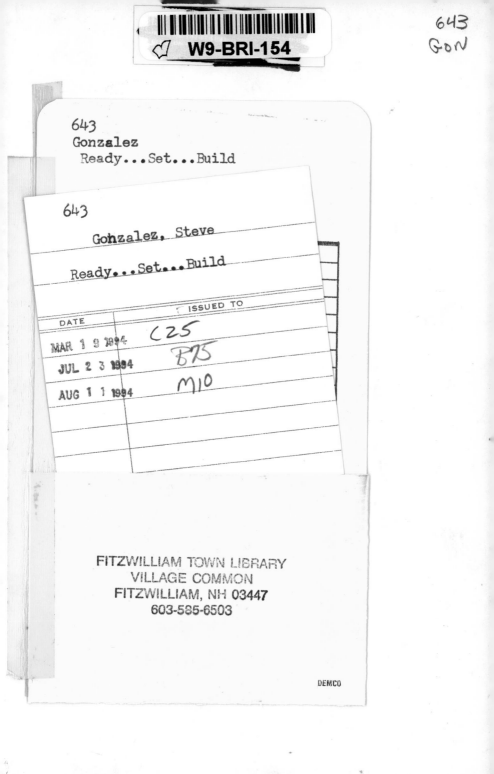

Ready...Set...Build

A Consumer's Guide to Home Improvement Planning & Contracts

By Steve Gonzalez, C.R.C.

Women's Publications
Fort Lauderdale, Florida

For Brenden and Anthony

Published by:
Women's Publications
13326 Southwest 28th Street, Suite 102
Ft. Lauderdale, FL 33330-1102 U.S.A.

Library of Congress Cataloging in Publication Data
Gonzalez, Steven R. - 1959
Ready, set, build: a consumer's guide to home improvement planning & contracts / by Steve Gonzalez. — 1st ed.
　 p. cm.
Includes index.
1. Dwellings—Remodeling—Planning.
2. Consumer education.
I. Title.
TH4816.G65　1993　643'.7—dc20　CIP 93-17327
ISBN 0-9628336-7-3　　$9.95　Softcover

10　9　8　7　6　5　4　3
Printed in the United States of America

■ CONTENTS ■

■ ACKNOWLEDGEMENTS ■

Special thanks to all of the tradespeople and professionals who shared their knowledge, expertise and time to help create this book. They include:

Diana Gonzalez, Paula Pierce, Pam Price, Joseph Pappas, Diane Lentini, Linda Muzzarelli, Chris Nicholson, William Malone, Marlene Vega, Alina Garcia, Garry Spear, Tina Chubbs, Carole Collins and Allen Pfenninger.

■ INTRODUCTION ■

This book was written for everyone considering a home improvement project.

My intentions in writing this guide are to help consumers become educated on proper contracting standards and procedures in order to protect themselves from various pitfalls.

It is my belief that with increased consumer education and communication between homeowner and contractor, a home improvement experience can always be a rewarding one.

Steve Gonzalez, C.R.C.

■ CHAPTER ONE ■

Getting Educated: The First Step

There are many reasons for deciding to do a home improvement. An addition to your family might have you considering an addition to your home, too. Maybe you have a great idea for a new kitchen. Or maybe you've decided your teenager really *does* need his or her own bathroom.

Whatever your reason, you may now be faced with deciding how to select a contractor, gather bids and negotiate a contract.

The best approach: become educated about various details of building and take an active part in planning your project. Get involved!

Books & Videos: The Tools of Education

Start by visiting your local library or bookstore and obtain books on home improvements by category, such as kitchen remodeling, bathroom remodeling or home additions. Look for titles written about the quality of materials, or titles which include chapters on material quality.

Many libraries also carry a selection of home improvement videos which they loan out. Videos are helpful as far as showing you how a job should be done, although most do not go into detail about the quality of materials.

Hometime® offers several excellent low-cost videos. You can obtain their catalog of available videos by calling 800-227-4888 or by writing to them at Hometime, Order Department RSB, 4275 Norex Drive, Chaska, MN 55318.

Materials: The Basis of Your Project

Materials make up the basis of your project, therefore you should begin by educating yourself about various products. For example, if you desire wood flooring, start out by visiting wood flooring manufacturers' warehouses or showrooms and/or writing to them for illustrated information packets and samples.

Most materials used in construction are stocked by several manufacturers and are available in various grades of quality, color and texture.

Lumber grades in particular are often disputed between owner and contractor or buyer and seller. Product samples are a good way of avoiding any disputes over lumber or any other materials to be used on your project. Be sure to hold on to the samples you choose for comparison with the materials being installed in your home.

Contact manufacturers for product information on tile, insulation, plumbing fixtures, doors, windows, carpeting and other materials your project requires. Learn how the materials are made, the proper procedure of installation and how to care for them after installation.

Ask friends and acquaintances who have had similar work done what they do and don't like about the materials used for their projects. Inquire about specific problems, if any, they have encountered. This is especially important with materials that receive a maximum of use, such as carpeting, faucets and doorknobs.

Quality

Quality can mean different things to different people. You may request a "quality" paint for the exterior of your home and be given one company's 5-year guaranteed, middle-of-the-line paint, when your idea of quality is another brand of lifetime-guaranteed top-of-the-line paint.

Being specific on your contract will help you to avoid this type of situation. Research the products and materials and request the exact quality you want.

Product quality differs from company to company. Brand names with good reputations for overall reliability and customer service are generally worth the investment.

Quality also varies within each brand name. Most every brand name product line has a good, better and best lineup. For example, Moen offers base model faucets in its Touch Control and Aqua Stream lines, higher quality models in its Chateau line, and more elaborate, top quality models in its Legend line.

Your decisions will have a lasting effect. This can range from having or avoiding the cost and annoyance of replacing faulty materials to the increased or decreased resale value of your home.

It is also important to monitor the quality of workmanship while your project is being done. If you cannot be there while the work is in progress, make daily visits to the job and make note of anything that appears incorrect to you. Communicate your notes with the contractor on a regular basis.

Warranties and Guarantees

Methods of installation may affect warranties and guarantees. Read them carefully and make sure you understand them — educate yourself. Call the manufacturer if you have questions regarding whether or not a certain form of installation will void the warranty or guarantee. Be sure the contractor's method of installation meets the requirements of the manufacturer. Written warranties, including duration, should be included in all contracts.

Specifications

Becoming educated about materials and appliances and being specific about what you want makes bidding "apples for apples" and leaves no room for error on your part. It also saves the contractor time and eliminates guessing.

Make sure to include the following when specifying appliances and/or materials for bids:

Make
Model/Model Number
Style
Size
Color or Shade
Weight
Thickness

When shopping for materials and appliances, be sure to inquire whether or not the items are in stock. It is best to avoid requesting bids with items that are no longer being stocked by major carriers.

Be sure to look for clauses in contracts that state the contractor's right to substitute items "of equal to or better quality" or "their equivalent". A contractor's idea of quality or an equivalent may not be the same as yours. Also, you may prefer a particular appliance's layout or features, only to receive one you don't like.

If a substitution clause does exist within the contract, make sure it specifies that the owner must be informed **in writing** before any changes of materials are made. Reserve the right to choose all substituted items with ample time prior to installation.

The Contractor

There are five essentials to look for when choosing a home improvement contractor:

1) Fully licensed or registered (city, county and/or state, as required).
2) Fully insured (worker's compensation, general liability, property damage).
3) Clean complaint record.
4) Established local business, good reputation with local supply houses.
5) Satisfied previous clients.

Confirm a physical address and local phone number for the contractor. Be wary of contractors offering P.O. box numbers or motel addresses as their place of business.

See Chapter Four for additional information on selecting a contractor.

Zoning Restrictions: Is Your Project Buildable?

It is essential to confirm that the project you have in mind is buildable with regard to zoning restrictions.

First, obtain a survey of your property (you should have been given a survey when you purchased your home). Building departments generally require surveys to be less than three years old, therefore most surveys will need to be updated. It is easiest and may save you money if you are able to contact the original surveyor to get an update.

Next, make a trip to both your city or town and county building departments and find out if there are any new or existing restrictions that would cause you to be unable to build the project. Obtain copies of zoning rules and building codes for your city or town and county, as well as plans for future roads and growth expansion.

Generally, zoning rules govern what percentage of a parcel of land may be developed and what percentage is to be landscaped.

Some typical reasons for zoning restrictions are: easements, dedications, rights-of-way and setbacks. Setback requirements limit how close to a property line, road or easement a project may be built.

Although a common building request, many municipalities will not allow additions to be used as rental space. In some areas it is illegal to develop a basement apartment. Check on restrictions **before** you have drawings or blueprints made.

There may also be an Architectural Control Board in your municipality which must approve your project plans or drawings before a permit will be issued. If so, gather information on the procedures and requirements.

If the project you want to build is not allowable due to zoning restrictions, you may want to consider an alternative. For example, an addition which has dimensions too deep or wide may be allowable as a two-story addition with reduced floor dimensions.

Another alternative is to appeal to your local zoning board for a variance. When making an appeal, you will be required to attend a hearing. Gaining support of neighbors who are not opposed to your construction project plans may be useful at this point. Reasonable requests for variances are often granted. Confirm how long it will take to get the results of the variance request.

NOTES:

_____

_____

_____

_____

_____

_____

_____

_____

_____

_____

_____

_____

_____

_____

■ CHAPTER TWO ■

The Lien Law:
What It Is and
How It Affects You

The Lien Law

What is the Construction Lien Law?

The Construction Lien Law allows persons who have performed labor and/or provided building materials on or for your property and have not received payment for their goods and/or services to make legal claim for payment against your property.

How can you protect yourself?

By becoming educated and understanding the law.

1) Be certain a Notice of Commencement (or equivalent document, depending on state law) has been filed before the start of your remodeling or construction project. The Notice of Commencement form is provided where building permits are issued for your area. This form must be recorded with the Clerk of the Circuit Court in the county where the property is undergoing construction or remodeling. A certified copy should be posted at the job site (or an affidavit stating it has been recorded with a copy of the Notice of Commencement attached). Make sure all of the information listed on the Notice of Commencement is correct. The Notice of Commencement identifies:

   A) property owner
   B) location of property

C)   contractor
D)   description of project
E)   lender
F)   surety
G)   amount of bond, if applicable
H)   date of commencement

Failing to record a Notice of Commencement or obtaining one with incorrect information may add to the possibility of having to pay twice for labor or materials, and/or may prevent the passing of code inspections.

2)   **Never** make a payment without receiving a release of lien from the builder, suppliers and subcontractors, as applicable.

What is a Notice to Owner?

Contractors or suppliers will usually send you a Notice to Owner form once they are contracted to supply materials or labor for your project. It is not a lien on your property, however it is a legal document advising you that they are supplying materials and/or labor for your project. Be advised that not all states require Notices to Owner to be sent to homeowners. Always request releases of lien from any firm or individual who sends you a Notice to Owner.

Who is responsible for obtaining Releases of Lien?

You may want to stipulate on the project contract that the contractor is responsible for providing you with all releases of lien. If this clause is not included, it may become the homeowner's responsibility.

What is a Partial Release of Lien?

As each payment is made for a particular part of your job, you should receive a partial release of lien for all materials and labor to date. Upon completion of the entire project, make sure you receive a final release of lien.

In what instance could a Lien be imposed against your property?

Let's say, for example, that you hire a contractor for a $10,000 bathroom remodeling project. You pay the contractor the $10,000 in full, but he neglects to pay three material suppliers who sent supplies used on your project. There is no clause in your contract stating that the contractor is responsible for providing you with releases of lien, and the contractor has neglected to supply you with them. Each supplier who has not been paid may then place a lien against your property until they have been paid.

How does a lien affect you legally?

You cannot sell or transfer ownership of your property until all outstanding liens have been paid. You may also find you are unable to refinance your mortgage or secure a home equity loan if you have an outstanding lien or liens.

In rare instances, property owners with outstanding liens may be required to sell their property to satisfy them.

In General

Lien law provisions vary from one state to another. To confirm lien law provisions in your state, contact the Division of Consumer Services or the Real Estate Commission for your area.

It is important to include a release of lien clause in your contract. This clause should state that the contractor must furnish you with a partial release of lien from all subcontractors and suppliers upon each payment, with a final release of lien from all subcontractors, suppliers and the contractor himself upon completion of the project and final payment. Remember not to make any payments without receiving lien releases.

A sample copy of a final release of lien is provided on the following page.

FINAL RELEASE OF LIEN

      KNOWN ALL MEN BY THESE PRESENTS, that the undersigned, _____, for the sum of _____(_____) lawful money of the United States of America, to the undersigned in hand paid, the receipt whereof is hereby acknowledged, does hereby waive, release, remise and relinquish the undersigned's right to claim, demand, impress, or impose a lien or liens in the sum of $_____ for work done or materials furnished (or any other kind or class of lien whatsoever) up to the _____ day of _____, 19___ on the property described on Exhibit "A" attached hereto and made a part hereof.

   EXHIBIT A

_____

_____
COMPANY NAME

_____

_____
BY:_____

_____

_____
TITLE (President or V.P.
or Owner or Partner)

Signed, sealed and delivered
in the presence of:

_____

(Witness)

_____

(Witness)

Reference:

Check Number: _____

Check Date: _____

NOTES:

_____

_____

_____

_____

_____

_____

_____

_____

_____

_____

_____

_____

_____

_____

■ CHAPTER THREE ■

Your Project Budget: Loans & Financing

Loan Shopping

Surveys show that the majority of homeowners do not actively shop around when seeking home improvement loans. Yet thousands of dollars can be saved simply by doing some research.

The three main things to consider when shopping for a home improvement loan are:

1) interest
2) fees
3) percentage of allowable tax deduction

There are many types of loans available, some more advantageous than others. Here are the most common ones:

Home Equity Loans

Home equity loans are designed to allow homeowners to borrow monies on the equity in their home. The equity is calculated by deducting the mortgage amount (if any) from the home's present market value, which is usually figured by a property appraiser hired by the mortgage company.

Other factors affect the actual amount loaned. Most banks today also prefer that a homeowner's total monthly payments (car, insurance, utilities, mortgages, etc.) are equal to 40% or less of their net monthly income. Many banks now require a minimum income level no matter what equity you have.

The interest rate on a home equity loan depends mainly upon the prime rate. Then the bank adds percentage points (generally averaging anywhere from one to four) above prime. Different banks offer different rates — one bank may offer two points over prime, while another may offer four. A two-point percentage difference can equal thousands of dollars over the life of a loan.

Interest charged on home equity loans is fully tax deductible — an attractive feature, especially on larger home improvement projects — so long as the homeowner's total debt for all properties owned does not exceed the amount of $1.1 million (this won't be a problem for most of us).

Whether to secure a fixed rate loan or adjustable rate loan should also be carefully considered. Adjustable rates fluctuate with the prime rate — and go up and down accordingly. Confirm the "cap," or rate that an adjustable rate loan cannot exceed, regardless of the prime rate. To receive a copy of the "Consumer Handbook on Adjustable Rate Mortgages," send fifty cents to: Consumer Information Center, Department 423Z, Pueblo, CO 81009.

Fees charged for a home equity loan include the cost of a title search, a credit check, appraisals and points. Each bank may require different fees for these services. Here again, the consumer should shop around.

Home Equity Lines

This type of loan is actually an approved credit line. The amount borrowed is comparable to that of a home equity loan, the only difference being that with a home equity line you receive a checkbook and write checks out as you need them, rather than receiving the money as one lump sum.

An advantage to this type of loan is the way in which interest is charged. You are only charged interest on the amounts you write checks for. This is beneficial for projects requiring several months for completion, or time and materials contracts.

Interest rates on home equity lines typically adjust monthly. Fixed rate home equity lines are also available, though generally at a higher rate.

Fees for this type of loan are comparable to those for a home equity loan, and usually include the cost of a title search, credit check, appraisals and points.

Home Improvement Loans

These type loans range from a minimum of approximately $5,000 up to as much as 90% of the appraised value of a home, with varying interest rates. They are 100% tax deductible when secured by the home. The payback period is generally only five to seven years, which may result in rather high monthly payments.

Fees for this type of loan are normally limited to a credit check — making its fees less than those of a home equity loan.

Life Insurance

Whole life insurance may be another loan source possibility. Rates are generally low and an amount up to the full cash value of the policy may be borrowed. The interest is 100% tax deductible.

HUD - FHA Loans

These type loans are offered by banks participating in the Federal Housing Administration (FHA) program. Through this program, the FHA insures loans for home improvements. The down payment and interest rates are commonly lower than those of conventional home improvement loans. Fees include a credit check, appraisals, closing costs, insurance and points.

401k Plan

Depending on the trust document of your 401k plan, you may be able to borrow money from the plan. The payback period is usually 5 to 10 years. All interest paid on the loan is deposited into your own account, so you actually pay yourself the interest. Interest rates are generally slightly over prime and there are no fees.

In the event you leave the company with which your 401k plan is set up prior to paying off the loan, you must either forfeit the monies remaining or pay back the full amount in order to roll over the 401k.

Loans Through Contractors

As with any loan, thoroughly check interest rates and fees on loans offered by contractors through banks or other financial institutions. Don't assume the contractor will find you the best deal.

What To Look Out For

Unsecured Personal Loans

Unsecured personal loans carry a harsh payback period, generally only 3 to 5 years (up to 4 years less than most home improvement loans). Rates for this type of loan are almost always higher than a secured home improvement loan. Another downside: unsecured personal loans are not tax deductible.

Balloon Payment Loans

These type loans require that interest be paid back over a set period of years. At the end of that period, the loan balloons, requiring the full amount of the principal to be paid as one sum. What happens if, due to whatever reason, you find you are unable to secure a new loan when your first loan balloons? What would you do in the event the amount of equity in your home had decreased, leaving you without sufficient monies to cover the balloon payment? These type loans warrant very careful consideration.

Cash Payments

Cash payments are never a good idea. Cash should be turned into money orders or deposited into a financial institution and paid out in the form of checks or drafts. This offers a valid form of documentation that a payment or payments were made.

NOTES:

_____

_____

_____

_____

_____

_____

_____

_____

_____

_____

_____

_____

_____

■ CHAPTER FOUR ■

Coordinating With An Architect

At some point during the home improvement planning process, you may need to obtain project plans or drawings.

Projects needing changes and/or additions to plumbing, electrical, mechanical or the structure of a residence generally require drawn plans. These plans are submitted to your local building and zoning department to obtain necessary permits.

At this stage, homeowners generally interview architects, hire one, have a set of drawings made, and finally contact contractors to seek bids. A more effective alternative is to coordinate the services of the architect and contractor, as follows:

1) Confirm through local building and zoning departments that your project is buildable according to code rules.

2) Hire an architect for a **preliminary** set of drawings.

3) Interview contractors who are willing to work with your architect.

4) Consult with the contractor you choose on price and schedule, then return to the architect with any changes for a final drawing to your specifications and budget.

5) Coordinate a meeting with the owner(s), architect and contractor prior to the final plans being drawn.

These steps afford you the opportunity to take an active part in planning your project.

It is important to note that not all contractors will work with unfamiliar architects, for legal or other reasons. This may account for the rapid increase in "design-build" firms.

These firms coordinate every phase of a project, from design and drawing of the plans through to construction and completion, using the services of on-staff architects and builders.

Although design-build firms offer one-stop shopping for the consumer, they may limit your choice of materials and fixtures. This is due to the fact that most design-build firms order supplies from a set group of suppliers.

When using a design-build firm, the consumer should continue to oversee the project, making sure everything appears correct and making notes of anything that doesn't.

Another option available to homeowners is to have the contractor, if qualified, draw your preliminaries (many experienced contractors draw both preliminary and final plans). This can be money-saving and effective, especially when you are doing an improvement for space, rather than design.

One advantage of having a qualified contractor draw your plans is his hands-on experience not only with the structuring of projects, but also with building materials and costs, thereby making him well equipped to provide you with a plan that realistically meets both your needs *and* your budget.

Final plans drawn by a contractor may need to be reviewed and sealed by a registered engineer before being submitted for a building permit. If so, confirm the cost of the engineer's services and be sure it is included in the contract agreement.

Whether you decide to use the services of an independent architect, a design-build firm or the contractor for your drawings, ask for references and request to see drawings of previous projects similar to yours.

NOTES:

■ CHAPTER FIVE ■

Choosing A Contractor

Many people rely on friends and acquaintances for referrals of contractors. This is an effective way to obtain names of contractors to work with. The opportunity to see completed work first hand and get an honest opinion from someone you know about the contractor and every aspect of a home improvement project saves a lot of time and energy that would be spent shopping around for a competent, reliable and trustworthy contractor.

Whether you contact a contractor through a referral from a friend or by any other means, do not be in a hurry to make a decision. Meet with a minimum of three contractors to discuss your project and to get a general impression of which contractor you would be able to communicate with best. Use professional courtesy and avoid confusion by scheduling each contractor to meet with you at a different time.

Many contractors offer free estimates. Confirm estimate charges, if any, with each contractor before they meet with you to discuss your project.

When each contractor comes out for the initial visit, be prepared with a list of items to be discussed, plans or drawings of the work and any ideas you have in design, including magazine clippings.

Be frank and to the point as you question each contractor's abilities and experience. A contractor is a consultant as well as an estimator, thereby you should obtain as much information as possible pertaining to your specific project. Take notes.

Ask each contractor to provide you with a copy of his license or registration and insurance(s). Also request copies of bond certificates, if bonded. Check the documents for validity. Be thorough. Call the insurance agent or carrier to confirm the insurance is in effect and when it expires.

Request a business card. Usually the license number of the contractor is printed on his card (in many states license numbers are legally required to be printed on **all** stationery and advertising).

Call the applicable licensing facility with each contractor's license or registration number and name. Ask if each contractor has had any prior complaints filed against him or penalties imposed on his license.

Request a list of references. This is important whether or not a contractor was referred by a friend. When calling references supplied by a contractor, inquire about the contractor's financial responsibility on the project. Ask whether or not releases or waivers of lien were received, what percentage of the total contract price was required prior to the contractor commencing the project, and what percentage of the contract amount was retained at the end of the project.

Schedule appointments with referrals and request to visit the homes to see the quality of work done by each contractor. Choose referrals whose projects are similar to yours. If possible, visit a project in progress. After meeting with two or three references, you should be able to make an educated decision on which contractor to use for your home improvement project.

Remember:

When considering a home improvement contractor:

▸ Ask for a copy of city or town, county and state licenses or registration, as applicable. Your city, town or county building department or State Department of Professional Regulation can confirm this information. Be sure to get a copy of the confirmation in writing.

▸ Request a copy of the contractor's insurance and bond certificate, if bonded. Confirm the dates of expiration with the agent or carrier.

▸ Find out how long the contractor has been in business locally. Request a business card.

▸ Check with local building supply houses the contractor uses regarding the contractor's reputation in the industry and ability to pay material bills. They may also be a source for references.

▸ Request a financial statement from the contractor. You may also inquire about financial status through various credit sources.

▸ Contact your local Better Business Bureaus, building associations and consumer protection agencies, as well as your State Department of Consumer Services and the Department of Professional Regulation. Inquire about complaints, fines, suspensions or other reprimands, if any, which the contractor has received. Ask whether any problem situations are still unresolved.

▶ Ask for references of previous clients. Contact the references and ask specific questions regarding timeliness, response to concerns and requests, job clean up and overall quality of the job from their perspective. Ask to see the completed project. Your idea of a job well done may differ. Try to visit a job in progress.

▶ Inquire about employees and subcontractors scheduled to work on your project. Ask the contractor to provide copies of their licenses and insurance.

▶ Try to get a general impression of the contractor. Do you like him? Is he knowledgeable? Does he answer your questions directly? Does he appear to be organized and a good businessman?

▶ Take note as to the appearance of the contractor and his employees. Do they appear to be neat, orderly, courteous, professional and trustworthy?

Several associations offer informative consumer brochures on selecting a qualified contractor. Listed here are just a few:

The National Association of Home Builders Remodelors Council offers a free eight page pamphlet with suggestions on what consumers should look for when interviewing and contracting with a remodeler. It's titled "How To Find A Remodeler Who's On The Level" and is available by sending a self-addressed, stamped #10 envelope to: NAHB Remodelors Council, 1201 15th St., N.W., Washington, D.C. 20005.

The National Kitchen and Bath Association (NKBA) can provide you with a directory of its member contractors in your area qualified specifically in kitchen and bathroom remodeling. Write to them at 687 Willow Grove Street, Hackettstown, NJ 07840, or call them toll-free at 1-800-FOR-NKBA.

The National Association of the Remodeling Industry (NARI) offers a brochure titled "Selecting a Professional Remodeling Contractor." To receive a free copy, send a self-addressed, stamped #10 envelope to: NARI, 4301 North Fairfax Drive, Suite 301, Arlington, VA 22203 or call 703-276-7600.

NOTES:

_____

_____

_____

_____

_____

_____

_____

_____

_____

_____

_____

_____

_____

_____

■ CHAPTER SIX ■

The Contract

In the building profession, a contract is generally defined as a legal document between the contractor and owner(s) of a property where one party agrees to perform labor and/or services and/or supply necessary materials to complete a project and the other party agrees to make payment for same. In many states, contracts are legally required.

It should be noted that proposals and contracts are often one in the same. When issued separately, their content and specifications should be checked to be sure they are identical. The following categories should be included:

Specifications

Discuss with the contractors any specifications pertaining to your project which you feel should be included in writing. Specifications are any and all items you wish to be noted on the contract.

If you are not using an architect, your list of specifications should be given to each contractor upon his initial visit so that he may properly price the job.

Add to your specifications list a request for both partial and final releases of lien from major suppliers and all subcontractors.

Be sure the contract states that the contractor will be the receiver of any and all permits and variance approvals.

Make certain you provide each contractor with a final

list of specifications and purchase allowances or model numbers. This will ensure proper bidding guidelines and allow the contractors to bid comparatively.

Ask each contractor to supply you with product samples or brochures with the written proposal. Hold on to the product samples you are given to compare with the actual products provided to you at the time of installation.

Allowances

Contracts with allowances included in the price afford you the opportunity to shop for and choose fixtures of your own choice. These allowances also give you the breakdown you need to see how much money is being spent on fixtures.

For example: for a bathroom remodeling project, you may request allowances for plumbing fixtures, tile, electrical fixtures, mirrors, wallpaper, cabinets, shower doors, towel bars and other bath fixtures.

In the event the amount of money paid for the allowances exceeds the amount specified in the contract, the amount in excess is due to the contractor. Accordingly, if the amount of money paid for the allowances is less than was specified in the contract, the customer should receive the difference as a refund (provided there are no other arrangements in writing).

Contractors generally prefer to purchase the allowance items on their account(s), thereby keeping the project on schedule and coordinating measurements and specifications of the fixtures being selected.

If you decide to choose your own fixtures and let the contractor do the purchasing, he may charge you an additional handling charge for purchase, pickup and delivery. Many contractors offer their contractor discounts to homeowners, therefore, after deducting any handling charges, you may find you are still getting the best price on the fixtures.

If you decide not to have purchase allowances, make sure the contractor specifies in the contract the fixtures (including brand name, color or shade, model and model number) to be used on your project.

Project Schedule

Ask each contractor how much time is needed to submit the proposal for your project and on what date the work can be commenced. Inquire about other jobs the contractors are currently working on.

Confirm that the contractor you choose is readily available to commence your project with full intentions of starting and supervising your project on the commencement date listed on the contract.

If you've hired an architect, inform the contractors that you will schedule a meeting between homeowner, architect and contractor prior to the signing of the contract and job commencement. This is an important part of your project planning. Having two professionals consulting about your project with you prior to commencement can save you time, money and aggravation. Architects are design professionals, while most contractors are concerned with the physical development of projects, the cost of materials, labor and numerous other factors. Coordinating their services will help keep your project on schedule.

Your project may require interior design, landscape design, or other design services. Be sure to consult with the tradesperson who will be performing the design work before your draftsperson completes your plans. This can also help you avoid delays in your project schedule.

Duration of Project

Discuss the estimated duration of project with the contractor. Request a date of completion in the written proposal.

A clause may be added for penalties when a project is completed after the completion date listed on the contract. Penalties may then be assessed, as long as the reason for late completion is not listed as an exception (weather, acts of public authority, etc.) in the contract. Keep in mind that if you request a penalty for late completion, the contractor may request a bonus for early completion.

Change Orders

Control your budget. Proper planning of the project will eliminate the need for extras or change orders, which can be expensive. Written change orders and extras, including prices, should be signed for by both the owner(s) and contractor prior to their production.

Draw Schedules

On small jobs (under $10,000), many contractors require up to a 50% deposit to commence work. On larger jobs (over $10,000), usually a 10-20% deposit is required as first draw.

When a contractor submits a proposal, the draws are scheduled (as needed) with a retainer (generally 10-20%) upon completion of the project. Some states regulate both the amount of deposit and the payment schedule through home improvement laws.

Be sure a minimum 10% retainer is held on the final draw until final inspection and satisfactory completion of all items noted on punch lists (lists of items that need to be completed, mainly detail work).

If, for instance, the contract amount is $100,000 and the project is a 2 bedroom/2 bath addition, 6 draws should be adequate. Draw amounts will vary according to type, duration and cost of a project.

Thoroughly inspect the entire project before signing a certificate of completion and making the final payment. **All** final releases of lien should be in writing and in your possession **before** you release the final draw.

The contractor should supply you with a final release

of lien and final invoice showing that the contract has been paid in full.

Remember:

▸ Before signing the contract, be sure all of the information on paper is to your expectations. If any aspect is unclear, call the contractor and/or architect and have them verify what it means. If you are still unclear about any part of the contract, you may want to consult an attorney. NEVER sign a blank or incomplete contract. Cross through all blank spaces that do not pertain to your job. Do not be rushed into signing. Obtain a copy of the contract for your records.

▸ Be sure all warranties and guarantees (including their duration) of both materials and workmanship have been stated in the contract.

▸ Your specifications should be included as well as the contractor's. The contract should state specifically the work being performed, the duration (including commencement and completion dates) of the project and should specify the types of materials (including brand, model, model number, color or shade, weight and/or thickness) that will be used.

▸ The allowances or model numbers should be listed with prices included. The total contract price and a detailed draw schedule must be included.

▸ A place for the owner(s) and contractor to sign and

date as acceptance of the agreement is generally located on the last page of the contract. The signing of the contract should be witnessed by one or two other persons or a notary.

► All change orders should be in writing and specific, including cost of changes or additions, and should be signed by both the contractor and owner(s) prior to their production.

► When dealing with "cost plus" or "hourly rate" contracts, obtain written estimates with maximum amounts allowable to be charged.

► Be sure the contract states that you will be released from all liens. Make certain to obtain **all** releases of lien with each payment.

► Confirm that the contract specifies the contractor as the applicant and receiver of any and all required permits for the project, not the homeowner. If neither is stated, do not assume that the contractor is the receiver. Get everything in writing.

► Make sure a clean up clause is in the contract. Clean ups should be done at regular intervals throughout the project, with a final clean up upon completion.

The following is a checklist of what should be included in a contract:

____ Name of Owner(s)

____ Permanent Address of Owner(s)

____ Phone Number(s)

____ Job Name

____ Job Address

____ Job Phone Number(s)

____ Total Contract Amount

____ Payment Terms or Draw Schedule

____ Acceptance Date

____ Company Name

____ Contractor Name

____ Contractor License Number

____ Contractor Address

____ Contractor Phone Number(s)

____ Commencement Date

____ Completion Date

____ Project Delay Clause

____ Lien Release Requirements

____ Cancellation Clause

____ Warranties and/or Guarantees

____ Statement that work performed will meet code requirements

____ Unforeseeable work clause (for example: leaking pipes or electrical wiring problems behind walls)

____ Substitution of materials clause

____ Financing Information, if applicable

____ Permit Requirements

____ Liability Clause

____ Arbitration Clause

____ Clean up Clause

____ Days weekly and hours per day when work will be performed

____ Termination Clause (in case of poor workmanship)

NOTES:

_____

_____

_____

_____

_____

_____

_____

_____

_____

_____

_____

_____

_____

_____

■ CHAPTER SEVEN ■

Comparing Competitive Bids: The Best Price vs. The Cheapest Price

Most contractors strive to submit a proposal with the best price, as opposed to the cheapest price. The best price is determined by considering the full scope of a project, carefully figuring in all costs from beginning to end, then adding a reasonable profit.

Bids from low to high can vary thousands of dollars. There is much controversy as to which bid should be taken — low, middle or high. In the construction industry it is the general consensus that middle to upper middle bids are generally the best. These type bids allow for labor and material cost increases and other unforeseen situations, helping to prevent the contractor from cutting corners to finish the job.

Bids that are too low are a red flag for a host of problems. These can range from the underpayment of suppliers or low wages for workers to contracts that are purposely bid low, only to find that numerous items were left out of the contract and now need to be added through change orders. This can be a very costly process, and in the long run may cost you more than the highest bid.

However, extremely low bids given by a highly reputable contractor may warrant asking if something was left out or misunderstood.

Being vague will cause you to gather bids that are not comparable. Being specific (colors, model numbers, brand names, etc.) will give you a more accurate bid and allow the contractors to bid "apples for apples."

Time and Materials Bids

In general, these type contracts are risky due to the time factor, which may encourage the work to be done slowly.

Time and materials bids are sometimes requested when a contractor can't determine the full scope of a project from reviewing heavily detailed plans, or when homeowners are doing part of the work themselves.

One of the few benefits of a time and materials contract is that you don't need to put down a large deposit.

In any case, time and materials bid contracts should include a maximum cost amount (cap).

Labor Only Bids

Labor contracts are good for small projects, although they are usually given by subcontractors to general contractors. This type of contract may be acceptable if you can coordinate the purchase and delivery of materials.

In General

Some projects are quicker and easier to bid than others. These generally involve window replacement, roofing, siding, driveways and slabs, or other jobs that are bid on a cost-per-unit basis. For example, roofing and siding are bid in units of 100 square feet, called "squares" in the industry. Concrete is poured by the cubic yard and finished by the square foot.

Additions and remodeling projects which require that the structure of a home be modified will take longer to bid. This is due to more extensive figuring and the obtaining of bids from subcontractors, when necessary.

The size of a building company may affect the bid amount. This is due to profit and overhead factors. A smaller company where the contractor does most of the work himself may offer a lower bid.

Discussing your bid directly with the contractor who will perform the work may help reduce misunderstandings.

When bids are submitted, always be sure they include the following:

Company Name
Company Address
Contractor Name
Contractor License Number
Contractor Insurance Coverage
Lien Release Requirements
Project Address
Project Phone Number
Name of Homeowner
Phone Number for Homeowner
Address of Homeowner
Guarantees/Warranties
Payment Schedule
Acceptance Date
Job Commencement Date
Job Completion Date

Project Delay Clause
Unforeseeable Work Clause
Substitution of Materials Clause
Financing Information Clause
Cancellation Clause
Liability Clause
Arbitration Clause
Permit Requirements
Total Contract Price
Allowances
Specifications

Confirm that the model numbers, brands and types of materials you requested are all properly listed in the bids.

Many bid proposals have a contract incorporated into them. Carefully read anything you are asked to sign. Never sign anything immediately. Don't be pressured or intimidated by anyone who tells you their bid is only good for one week.

Remember:

▶ Request that the contractor come out and personally bid your job.

▶ All bids should be in writing. NEVER accept a verbal bid under any circumstances.

▶ Do not accept bids over the phone for jobs that haven't been seen in person.

▶ Bids too good to be true usually are.

▶ Be sure the contract specifies which materials the contractor is to use and what specifications they meet.

▶ Ask for several references of jobs similar to yours.

NOTES:

_____

_____

_____

_____

_____

_____

_____

_____

_____

_____

_____

_____

_____

_____

■ **CHAPTER EIGHT** ■

Understanding The Subcontractor's Role

Subcontractors are generally hired and paid by contractors. They should not be viewed negatively, as they are usually specialists in their fields.

Just as a dentist refers patients needing braces to an orthodontist, a contractor subcontracts a roofer to do a roof. In both instances, the services of a specialist within a field of work are rendered.

It should be kept in mind that it is not unusual for a contractor with many years of experience to perform several aspects of a job, from drawing plans to setting tile. There are, however, very few contractors highly qualified in every area of repairs or improvements. Therefore the services of a subcontractor are often used.

Commonly used subcontractors are electricians, roofers, plumbers and tile setters, although they are not limited to these trades.

Ask the contractor you choose for the names of the subcontractors he uses, and to provide you with copies of their licenses or registration and insurance.

Ask the subcontractors how long they have worked with the contractor. Many times subcontractors are a good referral source regarding the contractor's reputation.

Inquire whether or not each subcontractor uses their own crew (or subcontracts the work again!). Confirm whether or not the subcontractors use day labor (these are generally unexperienced workers, paid on a daily basis).

Companies who hire this type of labor may refuse to accept responsibility for the actions of the laborers.

Partial waivers of lien and full waivers of lien should be received from all subcontractors. Be sure your contract specifies who is responsible for obtaining waivers of lien from the subcontractors, the contractor or the property owner. In almost all cases it should be the contractor.

Most homeowners don't want to subcontract any of the work themselves. A homeowner considering doing their own subcontracting should also consider the following:

• Scheduling and timing play important roles in subcontracting. Each aspect of a job is closely integrated.

• How will you coordinate the subcontracting without throwing the rest of the project off schedule?

• Doing your own subcontracting may require that you alter or delete the completion date requirements or penalty clause for late completion within your contract agreement.

• Will you always be on the job site to answer questions and make decisions?

• What will you do when the decisions you make affect other aspects of the job?

• Do you know how to handle material shortages, labor problems, errors and changes in design?

- Do you carry the same insurance coverages as a contractor, that will cover the subcontractors should they get injured on your property?

- If you hire a subcontractor who stops production, for whatever reason, and it halts the work of the contractor, what will you do?

- Will you be able to pay the subcontractors yourself on a weekly basis?

- Do you have the experience to determine if the subcontractors' jobs have been done properly?

- Will you have money readily available to pay suppliers who bring materials? (Most contractors have supply accounts.)

- Will you be on site to sign for supplies when they are delivered?

- Do you know how to check the quality of the materials and supplies that are delivered, in case you need to reject them?

- What will you do if you need to fire the first subcontractor you hire and hire a new one? The work done by the first subcontractor probably won't be guaranteed by the second.

- Will you be issued the same warranties from subcontractors as you would from a general contractor?

The advantages of subcontracting on your own:

1) You can negotiate costs (this can also be done before you sign a contract).

2) You have more personal control over the job (and a lot more responsibility).

3) You can interview and choose each specialist working on your project.

The best recommendation for most homeowners is to thoroughly check out the contractor they choose and confirm that the company is financially stable with a good reputation for quality work.

Should you decide to do any part of the project on your own, be sure it is stated in writing in the contract agreement.

NOTES:

_____

_____

_____

_____

_____

_____

_____

_____

_____

_____

_____

_____

_____

_____

■ CHAPTER NINE ■

Your Rights As A Consumer

Whenever consumers are sold a product or service they have various consumer rights. Home building and remodeling is no different. In most states, after signing a home building or remodeling project contract, the following applies:

1) You may cancel contracts which are signed at a location other than the seller's regular business address, except in cases where you have specifically requested the goods and/or the services, by midnight of the third business day after the signed transaction.

2) You may cancel contracts you sign with a door to door solicitor or contracts which will be paid in installments for more than 90 days, so long as they are canceled by midnight of the third business day after the signed transaction.

3) In the instance of an emergency home repair or repairs, where the owner specifically requests emergency service, the three day cancellation policy is not allowable.

In many states, general contractors are required by law to inform you of your cancellation rights and to provide you with a notice of cancellation form.

Should you decide to cancel your contract within the three day time period, be sure to send your cancellation notice by certified mail, return receipt requested. Keep a file with copies of all correspondence.

Before you hire a contractor, check to see if complaints have been filed against the contractor, whether or not there are still unresolved cases, and how long the company has been in business. To confirm this information, contact your local Better Business Bureau and/or state, county or local consumer protection agencies. The following pages contain a complete listing of state consumer protection agencies.

Alabama

Mr. Dennis Wright, Director
Consumer Protection Division
Office of Attorney General
11 South Union Street
Montgomery, AL 36130
(205) 242-7334
(800) 392-5658
(toll free in AL)

Alaska

The Consumer Protection Section
in the Office of Attorney General
has been closed. Consumers with
complaints are being referred to
the Better Business Bureau, small
claims court and private attorneys.

American Samoa

Mr. Tauivi Tuinei
Assistant Attorney General
Consumer Protection Bureau
P.O. Box 7
Pago, Pago, AS 96799
011 (684) 633-4163
011 (684) 633-4164

Arizona

Ms. H. Leslie Hall
Chief Counsel
Consumer Protection
Office of Attorney General
1275 West Washington St., #259
Phoenix, AZ 85007
(602) 542-3702
(602) 542-5763
(consumer info and complaints)
(800) 352-8431 (toll free in AZ)

Ms. Noreen Matts
Assistant Attorney General

Consumer Protection
Office of Attorney General
402 W. Congress Street
Suite 315
Tucson, AZ 85701
(602) 628-6504

Arkansas

Mr. Royce Griffin, Director
Consumer Protection Division
Office of Attorney General
200 Tower Building
323 Center Street
Little Rock, AR 72201
(501) 682-2341 (voice/TDD)
(800) 482-8982
(toll free voice/TDD in AR)

California

Mr. James Conran
Director
California Department of
Consumer Affairs
400 R Street, Suite 1040
Sacramento, CA 95814
(916) 445-0660
(complaint assistance)
(916) 445-1254
(consumer information)
(916) 522-1700 (TDD)
(800) 344-9940
(toll free in CA)

Office of Attorney General
Public Inquiry Unit
P.O. Box 944225
Sacramento, CA 94244-2550
(916) 322-3360
(800) 952-5225
(toll free in CA)
(800) 952-5548
(toll free TDD in CA)

Colorado
Consumer Protection Unit
Office of Attorney General
110 16th Street, 10th Floor
Denver, CO 80202
(303) 620-4500

Connecticut
Ms. Gloria Schaffer, Commissioner
Dept. of Consumer Protection
State Office Building
165 Capitol Avenue
Hartford, CT 06106
(203) 566-4999
(800) 842-2649
(toll free in CT)

Mr. Robert M. Langer
Assistant Attorney General
Antitrust/Consumer Protection
Office of Attorney General
110 Sherman Street
Hartford, CT 06105
(203) 566-5374

Delaware
Mr. Donald E. Williams
Director
Division of Consumer Affairs
Department of Community Affairs
820 North French Street, 4th Floor
Wilmington, DE 19801
(302) 577-3250

Mr. Stuart Drowos
Deputy Attorney General for
Economic Crime & Consumer
Protection
Office of Attorney General
820 North French Street
Wilmington, DE 19801
(302) 577-3250

District of Columbia
Mr. Aubrey Edwards, Director
Department of Consumer and
Regulatory Affairs
614 H Street, N.W.
Washington, DC 20001
(202) 727-7080

Florida
Karen MacFarland, Asst. Director
Department of Agriculture and
Consumer Services
Division of Consumer Services
218 Mayo Building
Tallahassee, FL 32399
(904) 488-2221
(800) 435-7352
(toll free information
and education in FL)
(800) 321-5366
(toll free lemon law in FL)

Mr. Jack A. Norris, Jr., Chief
Consumer Litigation Section
The Capitol
Tallahassee, FL 32399-1050
(904) 488-9105

Ms. Mona Fandel
Consumer Division
Office of Attorney General
4000 Hollywood Boulevard
Suite 505 South
Hollywood, FL 33021
(305) 985-4780

Georgia
Mr. Barry W. Reid, Administrator
Governors Office of
Consumer Affairs
2 Martin Luther King, Jr. Dr., S.E.
Plaza Level - East Tower

Atlanta, GA 30334
(404) 651-8600
(404) 656-3790
(800) 869-1123 (toll free in GA)

Hawaii

Mr. Philip Doi, Director
Office of Consumer Protection
Department of Commerce and
Consumer Affairs
828 Fort St. Mall, Suite 600B
P.O. Box 3767
Honolulu, HI 96812-3767
(808) 586-2630

Mr. Gene Murayama
Investigator
Office of Consumer Protection
Department of Commerce and
Consumer Affairs
75 Aupuni Street
Hilo, HI 96720
(808) 933-4433

Mr. Glenn Ikemoto
Investigator
Office of Consumer Protection
Department of Commerce and
Consumer Affairs
3060 Eiwa Street
Lihue, HI 96766
(808) 241-3365

Mr. James E. Radford
Investigator
Office of Consumer Protection
Department of Commerce and
Consumer Affairs
54 High Street
P.O. Box 3767
Honolulu, HI 96812
(808) 586-2630

Idaho

Mr. Brett De Lange
Deputy Attorney General
Consumer Protection Unit
Statehouse, Room 113A
Boise, ID 83720-1000
(208) 334-2424
(800) 432-3545 (toll free in ID)

Illinois

Ms. Drinda L. O'Connor, Director
Gov. Office of Citizens Assistance
222 South College
Springfield, IL 62706
(217) 782-0244
(800) 642-3112 (toll free in IL)

Ms. Sally Saltzberg, Chief
Consumer Protection Division
Office of Attorney General
100 West Randolph, 12th Floor
Chicago, IL 60601
(312) 814-3580
(312) 793-2852 (TDD)

Ms. Elaine Hirsch, Director
Department of Citizen Rights
100 West Randolph, 13th Floor
Chicago, IL 60601
(312) 814-3289
(312) 814-7123 (TDD)

Indiana

Mr. David A. Miller
Chief Counsel and Director
Consumer Protection Division
Office of Attorney General
219 State House
Indianapolis, IN 46204
(317) 232-6330
(800) 382-5516 (toll free in IN)

Kansas

Mr. Daniel P. Kolditz
Deputy Attorney General
Consumer Protection Division
301 West 10th
Kansas Judicial Center
Topeka, KS 66612-1597
(913) 296-3751
(800) 432-2310 (toll free in KS)

Kentucky

Ms. Nora K. McCormick, Director
Consumer Protection Division
Office of Attorney General
209 Saint Clair Street
Frankfort, KY 40601-1875
(502) 564-2200
(800) 432-9257 (toll free in KY)

Mr. Robert Winlock, Administrator
Consumer Protection Division
Office of Attorney General
107 South 4th Street
Louisville, KY 40202
(502) 588-3262
(800) 432-9257 (toll free in KY)

Louisiana

Ms. Mary H. Travis, Chief
Consumer Protection Division
Office of Attorney General
State Capitol Building
P.O. Box 94005
Baton Rouge, LA 70804-9005
(504) 342-7373

Maine

Mr. William N. Lund
Superintendent
Bureau of Consumer Credit
Protection

State House Station No. 35
Augusta, ME 04333-0035
(207) 582-8718
(800) 332-8529 (toll free)

Mr. Stephen Wessler, Chief
Consumer and Antitrust Division
Office of Attorney General
State House Station No. 6
Augusta, ME 04333
(207) 289-3716 (9 a.m.-1 p.m.)

Maryland

Mr. William Leibovici, Chief
Consumer Protection Division
Office of Attorney General
200 St. Paul Place
Baltimore, MD 21202-2021
(301) 528-8662 (9 a.m.-3 p.m.)
(301) 576-6372
(TDD in Baltimore area)
(301) 565-0451
(TDD in DC metro area)
(800) 969-5766 (toll free)

Ms. Emalu Myer
Consumer Affairs Specialist
Eastern Shore Branch Office
Consumer Protection Division
Office of Attorney General
Salisbury District Court/
Multi-Service Center
201 Baptist Street, Suite 30
Salisbury, MD 21801-4976
(301) 543-6620

Mr. Larry Munson, Director
Consumer Protection Division
Office of Attorney General
138 East Antietam St., Suite 210
Hagerstown, MD 21740-5684
(301) 791-4780

Massachusetts

Mr. Robert Sherman, Chief
Consumer Protection Division
Department of Attorney General
131 Tremont Street
Boston, MA 02111
(617) 727-8400
(information & referral to local
consumer offices that work in
conjunction with the Department
of Attorney General)

Ms. Gloria Larson, Secretary
Exec. Office of Consumer Affairs
and Business Regulation
One Ashburton Place, Room 1411
Boston, MA 02108
(617) 727-7780
(information & referral only)

Mr. Carmen Picknally
Managing Attorney
Western Massachusetts Consumer
Protection Division
Department of Attorney General
436 Dwight Street
Springfield, MA 01103
(413) 784-1240

Michigan

Mr. Frederick H. Hoffecker
Assistant in Charge
Consumer Protection Division
Office of Attorney General
P.O. Box 30213
Lansing, MI 48909
(517) 373-1140

Mr. Kent Wilcox, Exec. Director
Michigan Consumers Council
414 Hollister Building
106 West Allegan Street

Lansing, MI 48933
(517) 373-0947
(517) 373-0701 (TDD)

Minnesota

Mr. Curt Loewe, Director
Office of Consumer Services
Office of Attorney General
117 University Avenue
St. Paul, MN 55155
(612) 296-2331

Consumer Services Division
Office of Attorney General
320 West Second Street
Duluth, MN 55802
(218) 723-4891

Mississippi

Mr. Trey Bobinger
Special Assistant Attorney General
Chief, Consumer Protection Div.
P.O. Box 22947
Jackson, MS 39225-2947
(601) 354-6018

Mr. Joe B. Hardy, Director
Regulatory Services
Department of Agriculture
and Commerce
500 Greymount Avenue
P.O. Box 1609
Jackson, MS 39215
(601) 354-7063

Ms. Mattie T. Stevens
Consumer Counselor
Gulf Coast Regional Office
of the Attorney General
P.O. Box 1411
Biloxi, MS 39533
(601) 436-6000

Missouri

Office of Attorney General
Consumer Complaints or Problems
P.O. Box 899
Jefferson City, MO 65102
(314) 751-3321
(800) 392-8222 (toll free in MO)

Mr. Henry Herschel, Chief Counsel
Trade Offense Division
Office of Attorney General
P.O. Box 899
Jefferson City, MO 65102
(314) 751-3321
(800) 392-8222 (toll free in MO)

Montana

Consumer Affairs Unit
Department of Commerce
1424 Ninth Avenue
Helena, MT 59620
(406) 444-4312

Nebraska

Mr. Paul N. Potadle
Assistant Attorney General
Consumer Protection Division
Department of Justice
2115 State Capitol
P.O. Box 98920
Lincoln, NE 68509
(402) 471-2682

Nevada

Mr. Myram Borders
Commissioner of Consumer Affairs
Department of Commerce
State Mail Room Complex
Las Vegas, NV 89158
(702) 486-7355
(800) 992-0900
(toll free in NV)

Mr. Ray Trease
Consumer Services Officer
Consumer Affairs Division
Department of Commerce
4600 Kietzke Lane, M-245
Reno, NV 89502
(702) 688-1800
(800) 992-0900 (toll free in NV)

New Jersey

Ms. Patricia A. Royer
Director
Division of Consumer Affairs
P.O. Box 45027
Newark, NJ 07101
(201) 648-4010

Mr. Wilfredo Caraballo
Commissioner
Department of the
Public Advocate
CN 850, Justice Complex
Trenton, NJ 08625
(609) 292-7087
(800) 792-8600
(toll free in NJ)

Ms. Cindy K. Miller
Deputy Attorney General
New Jersey Division of Law
1207 Raymond Boulevard
P.O. Box 45029
Newark, NJ 07101
(201) 648-7579

New Mexico

Consumer Protection Division
Office of Attorney General
P.O. Drawer 1508
Santa Fe, NM 87504
(505) 827-6060
(800) 432-2070 (toll free in NM)

New York

Mr. Richard M. Kessel
Chairperson and Executive Director
New York State Consumer
Protection Board
99 Washington Avenue
Albany, NY 12210-2891
(518) 474-8583

Ms. Rachael Kretser
Assistant Attorney General
Bureau of Consumer Frauds &
Protection
Office of Attorney General
State Capitol
Albany, NY 12224
(518) 474-5481

Mr. Richard M. Kessel
Chairperson and Executive Director
New York State Consumer
Protection Board
250 Broadway, 17th Floor
New York, NY 10007-2593
(212) 417-4908 (complaints)
(212) 417-4482 (main office)

Mr. John Corwin
Assistant Attorney General
Bureau of Consumer Frauds
and Protection
Office of Attorney General
120 Broadway
New York, NY 10271
(212) 341-2345

North Carolina

Mr. James C. Gulick
Special Deputy Attorney General
Consumer Protection Section
Office of Attorney General
Raney Building
P.O. Box 629
Raleigh, NC 27602
(919) 733-7741

Ohio

Ms. Dianne Goss Paynter
Consumer Frauds/Crimes Section
Office of Attorney General
30 East Broad Street
State Office Tower, 25th Floor
Columbus, OH 43266-0410
(614) 466-4986 (complaints)
(614) 466-1393 (TDD)
(800) 282-0515 (toll free in OH)

Mr. William A. Spratley
Office of Consumers' Counsel
77 South High Street, 15th Floor
Columbus, OH 43266-0550
(614) 466-9605 (voice/TDD)
(800) 282-9448 (toll free in OH)

Oklahoma

Ms. Jane Wheeler
Assistant Attorney General
Office of Attorney General
420 West Main, Suite 550
Oklahoma City, OK 73102
(405) 521-4274

Oregon

Mr. Timothy Wood
Attorney in Charge
Financial Fraud Section
Department of Justice
Justice Building
Salem, OR 97310
(503) 378-4320

Pennsylvania

Mr. Renardo Hicks, Director
Bureau of Consumer Protection

Office of Attorney General
Strawberry Square, 14th Floor
Harrisburg, PA 17120
(717) 787-9707
(800) 441-2555 (toll free in PA)

Mr. Michael Butler
Deputy Attorney General
Bureau of Consumer Protection
Office of Attorney General
27 North Seventh Street
Allentown, PA 18101
(215) 821-6690

Mr. Daniel R. Goodemote
Deputy Attorney General
Bureau of Consumer Protection
Office of Attorney General
919 State Street, Room 203
Erie, PA 16501
(814) 871-4371

Mr. Robin David Bleecher
Attorney in Charge
Bureau of Consumer Protection
Office of Attorney General
132 Kline Village
Harrisburg, PA 17104
(717) 787-7109
(800) 441-2555 (toll free in PA)

Mr. Barry Creany
Deputy Attorney General
Bureau of Consumer Protection
Office of Attorney General
IGA Building, Route 219 North
P.O. Box 716
Edensburg, PA 15931
(814) 949-7900

Mr. John E. Kelly
Deputy Attorney General
Bureau of Consumer Protection

Office of Attorney General
21 South 12th Street, 2nd Floor
Philadelphia, PA 19107
(215) 560-2414
(800) 441-2555 (toll free in PA)

Ms. Caren L. Mariani
Deputy Attorney General
Office of Attorney General
Manor Complex, 5th Floor
564 Forbes Avenue
Pittsburgh, PA 15219
(412) 565-5394

Mr. J.P. McGowan
Deputy Attorney General
Bureau of Consumer Protection
Office of Attorney General
State Office Building
Room 358
100 Lackawanna Avenue
Scranton, PA 18503
(717) 963-4913

Rhode Island
Ms. Lee Baker, Director
Consumer Protection Division
Department of Attorney General
72 Pine Street
Providence, RI 02903
(401) 277-2104
(401) 274-4400 ext. 354
(voice/TDD)
(800) 852-7776
(toll free in RI)

Mr. Edwin P. Palumbo,
Executive Director
Rhode Island Consumers' Council
365 Broadway
Providence, RI 02909
(401) 277-2764

South Carolina
Mr. Ken Moore
Assistant Attorney General
Consumer Fraud and Antitrust
Section
Office of Attorney General
P.O. Box 11549
Columbia, SC 29211
(803) 734-3970

Mr. Steve Hamm, Administrator
Department of Consumer Affairs
P.O. Box 5757
Columbia, SC 29250-5757
(803) 734-9452
(803) 734-9455 (TDD)
(800) 922-1594 (toll free in SC)

Tennessee
Mr. Perry A. Craft
Deputy Attorney General
Consumer Protection Division
Office of Attorney General
450 James Robertson Parkway
Nashville, TN 37243-0485
(615) 741-2672

Ms. Elizabeth Owen, Director
Division of Consumer Affairs
Department of Commerce
and Insurance
500 James Robertson Parkway,
5th Floor
Nashville, TN 37243-0600
(615) 741-4737
(800) 342-8385 (toll free in TN)

Texas
Mr. Joe Crews
Asst. Attorney General and Chief
Consumer Protection Division

Office of Attorney General
P.O. Box 12548
Austin, TX 78711
(512) 463-2070

Mr. Stephen Gardner
Assistant Attorney General
Consumer Protection Division
Office of Attorney General
714 Jackson Street, Suite 700
Dallas, TX 75202-4506
(214) 742-8944

Ms. Viviana Patino
Assistant Attorney General
Consumer Protection Division
Office of Attorney General
6090 Surety Drive, Room 260
El Paso, TX 79905
(915) 772-9476

Mr. Richard Tomlinson
Assistant Attorney General
Consumer Protection Division
Office of Attorney General
1019 Congress Street, Suite 1550
Houston, TX 77002-1702
(713) 223-5886

Mr. Robert E. Reyna
Assistant Attorney General
Consumer Protection Division
Office of Attorney General
1208 14th Street, Suite 900
Lubbock, TX 79401-3997
(806) 747-5238

Mr. Thomas M. Bernstein
Assistant Attorney General
Consumer Protection Division
Office of Attorney General
3600 North 23rd Street, Suite 305

McAllen, TX 78501-1685
(512) 682-4547

Utah
Mr. Gary R. Hansen, Director
Division of Consumer Protection
Department of Commerce
160 East 3rd South
P.O. Box 45802
Salt Lake City, UT 84145-0802
(801) 530-6601

Ms. Sheila Page
Assistant Attorney General
for Consumer Affairs
Office of Attorney General
115 State Capitol
Salt Lake City, UT 84114
(801) 538-1331

Vermont
Mr. J. Wallace Malley
Assistant Attorney General
and Chief
Public Protection Division
Office of Attorney General
109 State Street
Montpelier, VT 05609-1001
(802) 828-3171

Virgin Islands
Mr. Clement Magras
Department of Licensing and
Consumer Affairs
Property & Procurement Bldg.
Subbase #1, Room 205
St. Thomas, VI 00802
(809) 774-3130

Virginia
Mr. Frank Seales, Jr., Chief

Consumer Litigation Section
Office of Attorney General
Supreme Court Building
101 North Eighth Street
Richmond, VA 23219
(804) 786-2116
(800) 451-1525 (toll free in VA)

Ms. Betty Blakemore, Director
Division of Consumer Affairs
Department of Agriculture and
Consumer Services
Room 101, Washington Building
1100 Bank Street
P.O. Box 1163
Richmond, VA 23219
(804) 786-2042

Washington
Ms. Renee Olbricht, Investigator
Consumer and Business
Fair Practices Division
Office of Attorney General
111 Olympia Avenue, NE
Olympia, WA 98501
(206) 753-6210

Ms. Sally Sterling
Director of Consumer Services
Consumer and Business
Fair Practices Division
Office of Attorney General
900 Fourth Avenue, Suite 2000
Seattle, WA 98164
(206) 464-6431
(800) 551-4636 (toll free in WA)

Mr. Owen Clarke, Chief
Consumer and Business
Fair Practices Division
Office of Attorney General
West 1116 Riverside Avenue

Spokane, WA 99201
(509) 456-3123

Ms. Cynthia Lanphear
Consumer and Business
Fair Practices Division
Office of Attorney General
1019 Pacific Avenue
3rd Floor
Tacoma, WA 98402-4411
(206) 593-2904

West Virginia
Mr. Robert J. Lamont, Director
Consumer Protection Division
Office of Attorney General
812 Quarrier Street, 6th Floor
Charleston, WV 25301
(304) 348-8986
(800) 368-8808
(toll free in WV)

Wisconsin
Mr. John Alberts, Administrator
Division of Trade and Consumer
Protection
801 West Badger Road
P.O. Box 8911
Madison, WI 53708
(608) 266-9836
(800) 422-7128
(toll free in WI)

Ms. Margaret Quaid,
Regional Supervisor
Division of Trade and Consumer
Protection
927 Loring Street
Altoona, WI 54720
(715) 839-3848
(800) 422-7128
(toll free in WI)

Mr. Eugene E. Lindauer,
Regional Supervisor
Division of Trade and Consumer
Protection
200 No. Jefferson St., Suite 146A
Green Bay, WI 54301
(414) 448-5111
(800) 422-7128 (toll free in WI)

Regional Supervisor
Consumer Protection Office
3333 North Mayfair Rd., Suite 114
Milwaukee, WI 53222-3288
(414) 257-8956

Mr. James D. Jeffries
Assistant Attorney General
Office of Consumer Protection
and Citizen Advocacy
Department of Justice
P.O. Box 7856
Madison, WI 53707-7856
(608) 266-1852
(800) 362-8189 (toll free)

Mr. Nadim Sahar
Assistant Attorney General
Office of Consumer Protection
Department of Justice
Milwaukee State Office Bldg.
819 North 6th Street, Room 520
Milwaukee, WI 53203-1678
(414) 227-4948
(800) 362-8189 (toll free)

Wyoming
Mr. Mark Moran,
Assistant Attorney General
Office of Attorney General
123 State Capitol Building
Cheyenne, WY 82002
(307) 777-7874

NOTES:

_____

_____

_____

_____

_____

_____

_____

_____

_____

_____

_____

_____

_____

_____

■ CHAPTER TEN ■

Common Questions & Answers

Virtually every homeowner has questions when embarking on a home improvement project. Here are some of the more common ones:

Q.

Do we have to move out while our addition is being done?

A.

The answer depends on the extent of demolition, how susceptible you or your family members are to dust, if security will be affected and how much inconvenience and lack of privacy you are willing to tolerate. The size and duration of the project are also factors to consider.

Q.

What do I do if I change my mind about something that has already been completed?

A.

Consult with the contractor and request a change order. The contractor should then submit in writing the cost of the change. The change order should be signed by both owner(s) and contractor.

Q.

The contractor we would like to use provided us with a copy of his insurance. We called the agent and were told his insurance is up for renewal. What should we do?

A.

Add a stipulation to the contract requiring the contractor to provide proof of renewal **as of the day of cancellation** of the previous policy before any further payments will be made.

Q.

Is it okay to use an out-of-state contractor for a local project?

A.

Yes, if the contractor has obtained all local licenses and full insurance coverage and meets any other requirements so that he may legally pull permits. Consider the following before hiring an out-of-state contractor:

1)   How will you see previous jobs done by an out-of-state contractor?

2)   Will the contractor provide you with names and numbers of previous clients as references?

3)   Can the contractor provide you with the names and numbers of previous suppliers?

4)   Are there any complaints or unresolved issues listed with the Better Business Bureau in the state the contractor previously worked in?

Q.

The contractor working on my home has requested a draw payment and has run out of release of lien forms. What should I do?

A.

Do not make the payment until you get the release. Lien release forms are available from most office supply stores (you may even want to keep a few on hand).

Q.

I signed a contract and paid a deposit, then decided I wanted to cancel. What should I do?

A.

Several points should be considered. The first consideration is when and where the contract was signed. In some states, if the contract was signed within three days of your decision to cancel and you did not specifically request the goods and/or services, you may be able to cancel the contract.

If it is past the three day period, you may want to approach the contractor and request cancellation. If, for example, you signed a contract, then were informed that your company was transferring you to another state in 2 weeks, you may have a valid reason for requesting a refund. However, if the contractor turned down other projects to commence yours and has already put hours into your project, you may have to forfeit all or part of your deposit. Consult your attorney.

Q.

My brother's friend does carpentry work. Is it okay to use him on my project?

A.

This is a personal decision. In general, it is recommended not to use the services of family or friends for home improvement projects. What will you do if the work doesn't meet your expectations and needs to be redone? Additional expenses and hard feelings are often the result. Considering how detailed the carpentry work will be may help you to decide.

Q.

Do all contractors have to be licensed?

A.

No. Many states don't require their contractors to be licensed. Some states require contractors to be registered. Check your state requirements.

Q.

What if I use someone who is uninsured?

A.

In the event you hire someone uninsured, you may become legally responsible for injuries and/or damage to personal property.

Q.

The general contractor I hired recently changed subcontractors. I requested license and insurance information from the new subcontractor and he told me he isn't licensed or insured. What should I do?

A.

Speak to the contractor. Most contractors carry insurance which covers all subcontractors. Also, the particular subcontractor may not be required to be licensed.

Q.

What is a Bond?

A.

Bonds are issued by surety companies, whose function is to guarantee completion of projects done by contractors. There are different types of bonds available. Bonds are generally posted for amounts equal to or greater than the full amount of the contract sum for a home improvement project. Some states' bond requirements, however, are for smaller amounts. Payment and performance bonds usually offer the best coverage. Confirm the amount before signing the contract.

Q.

How can a Bond protect me?

A.

In the event a contractor does not complete your project, the bonding company may be required to reimburse you the cost of the project or pay to have it completed.

Q.

Can any contractor get a Bond?

A.

If he qualifies. To qualify, a contractor must submit an application and supply the bonding company with license, insurance and financial information that meets required standards.

Q.

Should I require that the contractor I choose be Bonded?

A.

It depends. There are many points to consider, including the size of your project and the amount of money involved. Many states require bonds. Certain municipalities require a contractor to post a bond if he is not in business locally. If bonds are required in your area, ask for copies of the documents.

Q.

How long are warranties on workmanship?

A.

1 year in most cases, although they may vary. Roofing contractors generally guarantee their work for 5 to 10 years. Some contractors offer outside warranties, such as those which are available through Home Owners Warranty Corporation. For more information on the HOW Remodeler Program, call 1-800-CALL-HOW.

NOTES:

■ INDEX ■

■ ABOUT THE AUTHOR ■

Steve Gonzalez is a Florida State Certified Residential Contractor with over 15 years experience in the building industry. He has built 150 homes and has successfully completed over 100 home remodeling projects.